the woman who couldn't finish things

Sue MacIntyre

First published in 2021
by Stonewood Press
Diversity House, 72 Nottingham Road,
Nottingham NG5 6LF
books@stonewoodpress.co.uk
www.stonewoodpress.co.uk

All rights reserved
Copyright © Sue MacIntyre, 2021
The author asserts her moral right to be
identified as the originator of this work

ISBN: 9781910413333 (Paperback)

Represented by Inpress, tel: 0191 230 8104
enquiries@inpressbooks.co.uk
Distributed by NBN International

Printed and bound in the UK by TJ Books Limited, Cornwall

Designed and typeset in Sabon 11pt/13pt
by www.silbercow.co.uk
Cover illustration by Martin Parker

Contents

The woman who couldn't finish things	5
The first cup of tea	7
Deep fact	8
Peat smoke	9
Mimosa	10
Five in the morning	11
Dream conversations	12
'The ordeal of sleep'	14
Hydrangea petiolaris	15
Edyta in the garden	16
Storytime at Keats Library	18
Black armada	19
Walking behind you	20
Quickly	21
Persistence of silver	22
Boy	23
Punk	24
Gulliver nights	26
Gold	27
Baggage	28
Whippet on a train	30
Piano	32
Going north	33
Fountain farm	34
Shadow tulips	35
Maine woods	36
Apricots	37

Cooking	38
Linked images, with hands	39
The latest poem	40
Re: Stone	41
Small cart	42
Lost bells	43
Matt Miles, turned away from us	44
The pigeons	46
Normandy, 2001	48
Cimetière	49
Estuary	50
Maridiana alpaca	51
Museo	52
Blue beads	54
New Year days	55
Elinor, Eleanor	56
Nightingale	58
Thoughts about life after a birthday lunch	59
The autumn of things	60
The woman who couldn't finish things	61
Notes on sources of quotations:	65
Acknowledgements	65

The woman who couldn't finish things

She tried to imagine her life as a story
told by Chekhov...

she thought he would observe her
with compassion and a kind of

humorous detachedness, at times exasperation
and anger not let loose for long.

Sometimes her story would be bleak.
Chekhov would require honesty of himself

and require that she came to honesty too,
by the end of the story, if that were possible,

almost certainly too late. She would have
his full attention and it would be as if

his house party, sitting in the lamplight,
the beautiful maid offering them

tea and jam, and the portraits on the wall
in their gold frames were all listening too.

She thought the crux of her story would be
that she couldn't finish things

but still carried around a trail of half-read novels,
incomplete poems, good intentions.

He would notice how easily her real world
became pale, her energy distracted,

how she was not able to decide until
the moment was past what she wanted,

and was trapped in longing
for what she could not have.

But she knew he would show it was not
so much finishing that mattered,

it was the sap, the energy, her brain
whirring furiously while she had

no idea where it was trying to take her.
And there would be consolations

in his precision, his word's pace, turning
a non-happening into a happening,

so the smallest events would become luminous
in some way – like the landowner in his story

confessing he had not had time to wash
since spring, the water in his bathing place

in the river turning first brown, then indigo
around him as he soaped himself.

The first cup of tea

in a small white mug – Alfred Corry Southwold –
hot, dark. The best time of the day, its first kiss.
Propped up on a pillow and a yellow striped cushion,
contained, held still but full of crazy thoughts,
memory flutterings. Not yet launched into the day's
crowded indecisions, its shapes, how it can turn
round ninety degrees from any plan and while you're
still in bed you can see all this, its spiked flowers,
from a safe distance. Today when you doze between
sips, dreaming of postponing the day, the trees come
into the room, their steadiness, their roots holding
you still but their wild leaves and branches saying let
go, go wherever you want.

Deep fact

small pieces   like fragments of china   but
are they memory   or stories of memory
father   or story of father lifting me
onto his Steinway   mother who
alternates with aunt   a safe haven
in the war   (the burr of my Devon uncle's
voice   his billy cans of milk)

or stand-ins for mother   at school
Katie David   Frieda Lerich   almost mothers
did I lie down in the road   and howl
when the real one left   almost mothers
I couldn't quite hold close   whose names
I still hold close to me   are they stories

but the Parrots dorm   nine small beds
'is anyone awake?'   scent of wisteria
laid down   deep fact   whatever else
has happened   in a long life

Peat smoke

I'm pushed towards the edge
words cannot reach any more
where something is slowly unfolding

nearby is a kettle, beads of water
on a damp surface, a white caress

then sharpness in my eyes
at the back of my nose that
shies me away with pain

the opening out of times away
a most remote village, softly lingering

distance but somehow weighted for me
by ungovernable memories
that hold both love and tears

Mimosa

The time is always the same. I grope upstairs
in the dark. A street light is shining in
above the closed half-shutters

and tonight the wind is tossing and heaving
the mimosa – on our white wall
shadows flicker, grey leaves

restless – tangling in my mind
with Morandi's early morning trees,
their silvery haze of cross-hatching

among the dim house shapes of Grizzana
where he spent time
devoid of exceptional events.

I once sat staring at his images, wanting
to learn his world by heart, hoping
to find a way into his uneventful summers.

And I want to keep this sense of mimosa
gleaming in the street light,
billowing forward in the wind

over the dark road,
then watch its muted shadow
like memory on our white wall,

dim patterns of its leaves and blossom,
never still, forward and back,
and part of our room now.

Five in the morning

the silent kitchen   the Spanish jug
luminous   simple

a circle of   green painted leaves
round its shoulders

it's not at home here   in the
jumble of   magazines and recipes

on the table   not part of
the coterie of jugs   on the high shelf

facing this way and that
but growing out of   its own landscape

filled with rosemary cuttings
tufts   thickets   of rosemary

it talks to   the grey green spikes
they talk   to each other

it's dark outside   the black
vine weevil's in the privet hedge

Dream conversations

for Barbara Fussiner

How they jostle to come out over breakfast,
over the bitter coffee, the breadcrumbs.
We're half wrapped in sleep's blanket,

barely listening to one another,
but still we sit together, lumpy feet bare,
glazed eyes, fingers twisting locks of hair.

I say my son – his face white silver fringe –
when was he like that? tells me
he's in an Irish prison but laughs,

shrugs it off, says he's all right,
is coming home for the weekend
and I'm writing a press release about him...

You're not listening. I let it go and far off
you're saying that both our sons were to go
to such and such university in America

beginning with B but ended up going to
another university, also beginning with B.
This seems amazing to you.

And you're becoming the editor of *Vogue*
at seventy after a fall down an immense chute.
The interview went well.

We're each following the brightness
of our own balloon as it floats up
and shrinks into a blank sky

but there's a bond in sitting here and
not listening, as if our not listening
sets each other's bright dreams free.

'The ordeal of sleep'

after a painting by René Magritte

Vulnerable, her bare neck
   curves to her naked shoulder,
     her turned-away cheek –

this is the beautiful surface
   of her ordeal in sleep.
     On her dreaming neck

her black and silver hair is
   delicately cropped, hairs distinct
     as wood grain patterning.

Something muffled thickly
   in a draped cloth
     faces her

teasing, menacing her
   when she offers herself up
     to the turmoil of dreaming,

radiant victim of
   a cruel practical joke.
     Her neck stirs my pity for her

as I think of the bare necks
   of soldiers, their wounds,
     their military haircuts.

Hydrangea petiolaris

Out into the garden in your nightdress again early,
moving briskly – you can't stay away, so durable what's there,
steadying you, your eyes, all your senses. You look up into
the summer plane tree that draws you into its shadows

or sit still in front of a peony or cross the fat grass
under the apple tree to the hydrangea petiolaris by the wall.
You stare at it in the severe hope of a surprise
so you can judge if its greeny white flowers are

coming on, growing up, but perhaps could do better,
become lacier. Or are you waiting for an admonition
from the flower face telling *you* how to grow –

'this is unfurling, this is how it happens', perhaps
with an unsettling sense that this simple flowering
is beyond us, beyond our laborious self-cultivation.

Edyta in the garden

She bounds through the open front door,
   her vigour bounds with her,
     her laughter, her embrace,

her wide face widening, pencilled
   eyebrows alert. She shoots downstairs
     to throw off town clothes, pull on

old jeans and gardening boots, just pauses
   for black coffee, nothing else but black coffee,
     nothing else all day but perhaps

one more black coffee. She tumbles
   down the garden stairs, she says
     working in the garden is so relaxing,

she relaxes into it with furious energy.
   'Oh the little darlings' she says
     to the clump of daisylike stars, only

she knows the Latin name,
   she knows all the Latin names
     of everything in our garden.

When she attacks the trees and shrubs
   and leaves them gaunt and bony, we know –
     she assures us and she's right –

they will return to shapeliness within the year
   and when she sends us out for
      bags of farmyard manure quite late on

we know it will be spread in a trice.
   And just before she leaves she asks
      could she possibly have a clump of those

Erigeron karvinskianus (we call them daisies) for her garden
   and she wraps them in wet newspaper and
      beds them down carefully in her rucksack.

Storytime at Keats Library

There's a huddle of pushchairs,
fathers with kangaroo pouches and babies.
In the big room the storyteller with whoops
and shouts is out-singing the children...

Lives hardly begun, your unfinished life.
*The half-built houses opposite us stand just
as they were and seem dying of old age
before they are brought up...*

Your bed's been made up on a sofa
in the front parlour. You look out
at a grass patch and a few cabbage stalks,
so much more lively than your room
upstairs where you've become weary
of the pattern on your bed curtains.

You watch the passers by – they spill
into your letter-stories to your sister –
between twelve and one you've seen
*brickmakers ... old women with bobbins and
red cloaks and unpresuming bonnets...
creeping about the heath. Gipsies
after hare skins and silver spoons. Then
goes by a fellow with a wooden clock
that strikes a hundred and more ...
a lap dog ... a corpulent little beast
whom it is necessary to coax along
with an ivory tipped cane ...*
are you writing so copiously
to distract her from your other news
a slight return of fever last night?

Black armada

'There are too many – you need to look at
one or two to really see them.' So I took down
the postcards of Fresh Maine Blueberries,
the circle of Dutch musicians playing in lamplight,
the two old men chatting and smoking
in a Chinese teahouse, the small girl beside them
elbow on the table, reading her small book,
the velveteen rabbit
                              and left only
Keats on his deathbed, his white face pillowed
on dark shadow, *drawn to keep me awake –*
a deadly sweat was on him all this night,
and a fleet of black-sailed boats on a churning sea,
labouring uphill, a small armada which seemed
to be beating towards him, towards Keats.

Walking behind you

for Helen

I'm walking behind you girls, young women,
jaunty, stylish, new haircuts short,

who step forward staccato,
upward loops of voice, pick up

your baskets of children's homework,
reports and on to the next thing

as though the day's stepping stones
surface as you walk.

Leaving home,
goodbye to the nesting bed,

you break the threads
as if you know they'll mesh again,

tearing grasses whose juicy stems
are sweet to chew.

Quickly

for Grace

Because you have stamped hearts the size of small ladybirds
in their corners, and because the notes you have blu-tacked
round the house saying – by the phone, 'ring friends being

social is gr8' and, by the switch, 'turn me off when out of use'
and, by the fireplace, 'burn waste product it keeps U warm'
make us laugh and we guess you have posted them with a grin,

and I remember you once sent a valentine saying Love is Life
with nail heads drawn in each corner to drive your point home,
and it's all so throwaway, not thoughtless, and you're part

of a quick-message life, I think of Frank O'Hara – *In times
of crisis, we must all decide again and again whom we love* –
and among the clouds of stardust are *the extras who pass*

quickly and return in dreams saying your one or two lines
and, think 'quickly' is you, not fast like a speeding train
but quickly as in quicken, make and become alive.

Persistence of silver

Hardly a house for miles
then a sudden gasp of silver
birches, skinny dipping
frail by the road

and again, barely holding up
after the snow, their frayed tops
and horseshoe scars
in the blur of fir woods

and more, brittle,
sometimes bowed over
to the ground
by snow, their arms

broken or angled down
under the canopy of firs –
streaks of silver,
remote night survivors.

Later in blue and white sun
they rush past us again –
dazzling, waving their leafy tops
on the town green.

Boy

for Sam

Hard, hard, he whacks his stick
on the railings, drags it along,

climbs every step he meets,
has run-ins with each litter bin,

circles round again and again –
a small boy's eagerness to touch –

hugging lamp posts and peering up
to look for missing ships' crow's-nests –

wanting to hold and smell and feel
to try to get at what it's all about.

Punk

papier-mâché on glass bottle

You look surprised, disgusted
that someone has dressed you
in flakes of gay patchwork, flowery

as a flock of mother's hands, and given you
a white satin chest, sequin earring,
pink shell button under your chin –

helpless, straining transition
from your nursed bottle body to staring eyes,
safety-pinned nose and snaking hair –

half-mothered genie in a bottle erupting
into your own cloud of midges,
your body smell, your swarm of angry bees,

your battered papier-mâché head
growing away, no, yanked up
by your cruel hair.

In quiet classroom smells where
they're doing the Nativity bottle people
project and making of crowns,

this boy's veered to another crown –
sticking pipe-cleaner snakes
into a bald head

and beginning to peer out, creep out
under the safety net, his activity scroll
is childlike and indirect –

a picture of coal mining he said
where intricately drawn small people
are chopping each other up.

Gulliver nights

Worry dolls crawling out of the bag at night
sit on the edge of the bed gabble gabble.

Look at yourself, the shine of your nails
in the moonlight. The gabblers take over.

Nearer nearer the little ones come
swarming up over poor Gulliver.

I'm pinned down on the bed
I can't even move my head.

Their light ricochet of ice-like
shards stings my face,

their sounds
incomprehensible hubble bubble.

Insect minute men –
they think their tiny loudness

is soothing onomatopoeia.
Take me to your leader I cry,

please take me.
Use all your strength to roll me

onto your gigantic cart
and drag me there.

Gold

for Dan

On the flight coming back from Torino
someone showed you how to make it you told me
from a gold paper cigarette wrapping –
a spiky gold flower.

You gave it to me although
at the time I wasn't sure where
you were living, you'd only call in
five minutes at a time.

I must have kept it
because it was so delicate,
so personal and it reminded me
you're clever with your fingers

and as a child had once
walked up into a copse
and found some sticks
and woven a shelter –

not a wigwam, more rounded,
and so quickly – when I came you'd
almost finished and were stuffing
the gaps with leaves and moss.

That copse was on the edge
of a new development
just beginning to show
in gaps through the trees.

Baggage

They don't speak much,
sometimes they hardly say a word.

They sit there between us when we meet,
ranks of suitcases, heaps of bags.

The old porter has trundled up the thick brown
leather case – brass locks black letters,

the stuff of long journeys my father made
from Brighton to Ballachulish with the German nurse.

Others spent years in a container in Mile End,
sometimes taken out to air – one with blond skin,

another, the Revelation, blue with leather straps.
A small green sausage bag flung on top, careless,

was lent from friend to friend. You slip off
your half-empty rucksack, pile it on the heap.

They called you 'luggage,' those friends, do you
remember, when you'd had too much to drink?

The story made me almost weep with anger
at the casual way they labelled you.

There's a painful musty smell, almost solid
as we open up, begin. How anxious I've been.

Layers of old clothes, rugs, worn shoes,
more cloth – it was once like

cloth of gold when you were a child.
Did I ever tell you that?

Whippet on a train

Is it because you're so thin
that you slip easily in and out of my mind?
I watch you led down the carriage

by the woman with a great bush
of red hair – you are sleek
with sandy patches and grey patches

still a young pup with your
long pointed nose
and serious brown eyes.

I watch the aloof man
unpack your soft basket and
fold you up and pack you away

in it neatly, your pointed head
staring out curious,
your angular body quiet.

The woman and man talk to you,
they don't talk to each other.
I watch your interactions

and the quiet thought arrives –
I don't want a single thing
about you to change –

not one of your movements
is clumsy or ungraceful.
Is this what we mean by beauty –

when a being has arrived at
being completely pleasurably
enjoyably here?

Piano

i.m. my Father, Peter Willans

A solitary man in a trilby hat walks briskly towards a church.
A man comes down to breakfast in a green paisley dressing
gown and says 'who's been eating my brown sugar?'
A man lifts me up onto the shining surface of his piano
and plays for me. I am restless, fidgety.

I seem to come towards you by a zigzag path tonight.
A waking dream: I'm walking in a wood in autumn –
damp, layered leaves, stillness, a musty smell,
out into a clearing – misty lake – ghost space.
I look down into the water. Your strained loving face
is drifting on the dark shining surface.
You're a reflection too.

Going north

i.m. Chris Acland

Unseen by you unseen by you
silver gold trees,
long fields for striding in.

Unseen by you
bridges where every brick is clear,
a slender factory chimney

unravelling silver smoke.
The train slides through still autumn
going north.

The lid is off the world,
my childhood eye –
fuzz of autumn woods

you could have picked them up
those little trees
and put them down again

like toys on our kitchen table,
enamelled sheep
standing on their shadows

in their thousands
all all unseen by you,
so many years unbreathed by you.

Fountain farm

i.m. my Mother

You travelled with me,
kept close for my return home
and in the garden –

hot summer, bleak heat –
reached out to comfort me.
I pulled away, could not

rest against you. You drew back,
apologised – it left you hurt, both of us
hurt and something changed:

the farmhouse was not heavy
any more, not planted in the ground
but floating as I dreamed it,

grass grew under it where it hovered
though its face of rosy brick was
the same as it had always been.

I rocked with it, disembodied,
floating off directionless
in my dream and in my life,

could not get back to its solidness,
the low rooms that held me
throughout a bad summer.

Shadow tulips

pink and white
downside-up parachutes

lips opening
a baby's skin

pink with streaks like
fine cats' hairs

blurred sunsets
on shining green stems

their shadows
drained of flight

flopping open
on the dark table

small ghost boats
black stamens clinging

to drooping green stems
still a toughness

your profile as I bend
to kiss your forehead

Maine woods

I think of the woods again, the summer woods
and their darkness,

trees that stretch on and on and on, those
nameless thousands

crowding closer to the houses since
farming died away.

And though you know you're following a trail –
splashes of orange paint

on trunks of trees – there's a time you're
so deep in you know you're lost,

you're sure – no sky, heavy dense pines,
the forest graveyard

from some winter storm, trees crashed
across your path

and silence, not a living thing, not one bird
or crackle in the undergrowth.

It's from childhood – you'd turned round but
the face and hand you'd clung to

had gone and it comes back again,
a sharp sense of that desolation.

Apricots

Baskets, bowls of them arrive in the house. The ground
>   is covered with their soft shapes,

their blondness – some wasp-damaged or bruised,
>   some still a little pale.

We suck the juice, dripping –
>   what can we do with them?

Bake them, stew them very gently,
>   a little brown sugar? Lemon? A flake of butter?

Slow cooking deepens their colour, makes their sharp
>   sharper, frees their wild scent.

Cooking

In my unhappiness
I can only cook
and it works well
because I don't want food
I don't want to taste
each night this week
such a good meal

Linked images, with hands

This old cookery book – yellowing
   with flaked edges and austere recipes

withdrawn to a shelf low down
   where my hand reaches for its crumbling spine

and I hunt for the sugarless flourless
   Christmas pudding,

find the place and keep it
   with my index finger –

has a kind of reticence
   like a friend's modest gesture

when she reached into her pocket,
   a shy movement,

to bring out a dark freckled cowrie shell,
   offering it to me quietly

saying 'this is what they give
   as presents down there.'

The latest poem

You're the good one nudging up to me,
wishing you could have all my lap,
not quite plain, hurt a little

because I haven't given you everything.
When at last I turn to you saying
'Oh all right, come here then' (or perhaps,

if I'd been my grandmother's mother,
'If you can't be pretty, child, at least try to be
amusing', rearranging your collar

and pinning back your light brown hair)
I find you're more complete
than all the others

I've been struggling with. But no one
quite believes your quiet grumbling,
colourless, holding in your hurt.

Re: Stone

for Philip Pollecoff

Dear Philip – among all the lost property left at your house, you didn't by any chance find a small oblong stone answering to the description 'squint owl with lopsided eyes' or 'barn owl with a glittering claw'? A very small stone that might be the beginning of a poem? If you did and it hasn't been thrown away could you possibly bring it next week? Love Sue   Dear Sue – has the stone those words inscribed on it or is it an actual small stone? If it is a small stone the chances of it surviving are small. Please let me know the shape and size of the stone and I will have a look. Best Philip   Dear Philip – a small oval stone, say two-and-a-half inches long, with little veins all over it. If it is not on the table in your sitting room please don't bother about it. No the words are not inscribed on it. It's probably under some heap here. I think I can remember it enough anyway. Thanks Sue   (A few years later) Dear Philip – I wonder if the stone has turned up? If I could hold it and feel the veins all over it perhaps I could carry on with the poem where I left off. Please could you have just one more look. Best Sue

Small cart

    Everywhere – in and out of tables
among calves and ankles
        the tribe of thin ones, tailless ones –

    this one has filthy white fur, raw pink above
her eye, round her ear black sores,
        her face passive as if

    she's been in things we can hardly talk about
and she haunts us, lurking
        from taverna to taverna.

    One evening we catch sight of her
in the small lighted jeweller's shop.
        The jeweller bends down and

    gently clasps the cat's small skull,
holds her in a brief moment of intensity
        and drops a few food scraps for her

    on the shining floor. And later
we hear about the small cart, the contraption
        the jeweller made for a crippled cat –

    we hear the first part of the story, not
the ending – did it last for a day? Who pulled
        the cart for the rest of the cat's thin life?

Lost bells

This is becoming mysteriously out of hand – a poem,
    part of a poem about church bells

but Italian church bells, alto or basso, mellow
    not a bright cascade –

I'm searching for them in the anthology. The sound
    hung over a somewhere

that was squalid, run down, I remember – do I?
    Part of a longer poem.

I can see the place on the page. It's say two-thirds
    of the way through the book,

quite low down. The more I hunt the stronger the hunger
    becomes – velvety enveloping bells –

are they somewhere near Cattafi's olives – those
    sharp-faced little whores?

or perhaps they're closer to Pasolini's Pope –
    a greater sinner than you has never lived.

Matt Miles, turned away from us

in memory

You're leaning on the porch,
   shoulder against the white post,
      jeans yanked up by crossed braces,

right hand in your pocket.
   Your head is turned a little
      but not enough to see your face,

its aliveness, its sallow skin,
   your slightly bulging eyes.
      It's as though we've followed you

out there, the lure of your quiet voice,
   your back drawing us to you
      yet stirring our sense of exclusion.

Beyond in bleached out space –
   is it Vermont or the Hudson –
      what words, what theories

are patterned there, caught up
   in branches or deep grasses or
      among light unanchored houses?

Once a skein of geese high up –
   a tracery past belief – fed
      your thoughts of interdependence –

I think the meaning of the great single bird –
   the eye on my neighbour to the right front,
      the sound of my friends –

is in the patterns we form without knowing.
   But now you lean there
      and seem to be part of nothing.

The pigeons

i.m. Martina Thomson

One day you rang me
(your voice seemed to be coming
out of a slow dream but this time
with an anxious edge)
   to ask whether the pigeons
      had all vanished here too?

There were no pigeons
pushing and shoving on your
windowsill fighting for breadcrumbs
(were you half-smiling, leaning
   forward, arms stretched out
      into empty space?)

There were no pigeons
anywhere nearby. I said I would go
to the Square and look for them.
The top of the Square
   was still and empty,
      love messages

for Amy Winehouse were
stuffed into the bamboo collar
of the plane tree opposite
her house. When I scattered
   my crumbs, no thick flock
      of pigeons

tumbled from the trees,
there was no greedy fighting,
none. And when later they started
to drop down, when this time
  they all came back
    it felt like a reprieve.

Sitting at the kitchen table
now, sun pulsing through
the lids of my closed eyes
as it comes and goes,
  I remember how deeply
    you wanted life to carry on.

Normandy, 2001

As if it's a row of picture dominoes –
this is the sliding rain, this

the placid house, the trotting horse
on yellow sand, a baby's speckled sock,

a shining conker slitting its dingy case,
a willow tree, a flapping sole,

pram wheels, a rusty gun,
green lanes with lost soldiers' names,

the withdrawn strip of sea
where words recede.

I match the pictures, link
their patterns on the table –

the toil of naming them.
Our holiday – bright wordless world

where sentences slide down
into a ditch somewhere, back

in the war of the hedgerows
and names left by the dead.

Cimetière

She looks out, her small white face framed
as if from an upstairs window,
hemmed in by everlasting flowers –
A notre Grandmère, A notre Arrière-grandmère.

Names and faces are arrayed
like portraits on a piano –
*Famille Delpoux, A notre Papy, Ma Tante,
Regrets, Ses voisins et amis.*

Durable neighbours and friends
guard the father and aunt and send
their ornate little messages.
Family archaeology, village within a village –

the tombs, glittering black marble,
stone with pillars of stone, hold out against
the ebbing of life from the other village,
the deserting of the church.

I sense them in the dark, the families,
their still presence, their bleak community,
as we grope down the hard path between
the tombs by starlight, feeling for the step

to the croaking of a thousand frogs.
And I wonder again where
I want to be after life –
to put away the longing to be remembered

or remain in a small town by a neat alleyway,
visited from time to time with feeling?

Estuary

The late afternoon's brief lightening
brings out the birds again after the rain.

From behind the glass, in the warm,
we watch the swooping barn owl –

it's six o'clock, most often six o'clock –
scudding low over the fields hunting,

quick brown in the browning light.
When we come out, drawn out,

the sea birds are settling for the night
on the silver mud of the estuary

with a loud murmur, a hectic chattering –
shelducks, black-headed gulls, dunlins,

egrets, redshanks, oyster catchers...
It's the time of the birds,

the near-night is alive with them
and we feel smaller, wonderfully small.

Maridiana alpaca

The same   the baize-topped table
the leather box of games   at an angle
deep brown shutters   small wood blocks
to hold them in place   dark verticals.
At night we walk   from room to room

where the pink moon   placid   just past full
is a blur   through the mosquito gauze.
This moment   we're trying to hold it still.
Did someone say   the moon is moving away from
the earth? We're told there'll be more turbulence.

We meet our friends   talk about our hearts
near the edge   by the steep rough track.
The small dog disappeared one day
they think she sensed   it was time to die
and the big dog Bocchio   collapsed beside them

they were caressing him   a moment before.
The wolves are coming back   to the woods
three alpacas killed   the winter before last.
The hunters are shooting everything else
Neanderthals   is what Gianni calls them.

We walk from room to room   through the door the hillside
opens up to us   the yellow tracks   the sallow ground
the steep green hills and mountain radiant   we need them
to stay the same. In the valley silent cars are   small beads
shimmering along the road   on and on like distant news.

Umbria, September 2015

Museo

i.m. my sister, Judy Acland

White mist in the morning
holds the pale silhouette of an animal –
sheep goat alpaca – moving in it

The amphora revolves slowly
telling the same fragment
of the same story over and over –
the king of Ithaca disguised
as a mendicant is recognised
by his wet nurse Euryclea
as she touches the scar on his leg

Out of the dream-field's white mist
you come again –
I cannot touch you

White walls space – the guides
are bunched together chatting
or heads down in their books
sometimes they look up open-faced
like the reclining clay women
they sit among who lie back
on their urns or prop themselves
on cushions banqueting
their necklaces like little cakes

*You're picnicking with friends
in a circle, forks and paper plates
poised – your alert secret face*

Earthenware ash-urns have
griffin heads and mourning women
'the overabundant decorations
are not particularly well observed' –
their unruly figures
interpenetrate the living

Nearby are the cheap coloured
mass-produced urns
of poorer people the iron
grey kitchen set of the dead

*You're flopped down beside a friend
on a footbridge in Cambridge –
you look down softly
your hair half-hides your face*

Blue beads

for Margaret Bonfiglioli

I've turned away too many times. Now I sit
in your warm room, see a web of willow roots

in the straight-sided glass vase I gave you once.
You bring in sprouting hawthorn in a tin jug. It's February.

We talk about my sister, it opens out –
you make a link between us – you're wearing

the blue beads she gave you once, I'm wearing
a green dressing gown you lent me –

you look at me and say you like the picture.
Locked up feeling spills over –

sisters are side-by-side, so close
and not quite reaching each other.

February 1998

New Year days

The young doctor behind her kind glasses says
it's viral, there is no treatment, just rest
and plenty of sleep – a permission
in this small sheaf of days, the old year's leaves
still around, a hard permission simply to lie down,
    turn towards the dark and sleep.

War and Peace is on all New Year's day.
The world is full of butchers,
the house awash with intentions,
each new day a mirage in a wavering trail
of pots and pans and heaped up papers.
    I thought of trying something new –

living sentence by sentence, trying to dislodge
each sentence one by one, no plan.
Near the end of the day, as the French retreat,
Field Marshall Kutuzov hunkers down and waits.
He refuses to engage again. He doesn't want
    Russia to lose any more men.

Elinor, Eleanor

The walk was more of an amble – it was midwinter,
sunny though. Yes the sun was a presence and
there was fresh green some way off between the trees –

a sense of coming up for air. The trees were bare
yet there were colours and I was carrying colours
in my mind ... as we cut the corner at a bend in the path

I asked you if the letters of the alphabet were coloured
for you too. I told you A is red and E is orange/yellow,
I is silvery grey and T is green for me.

You said I'd never talked to you about it before.
Then what did you say – as far as I remember
 it was not clear cut – and did we talk about my cousin

Elinor or Eleanor – I can't remember just now how
she spells her name. One spelling makes her thin and pale,
wearing the other she is sunny and plumper.

She is wrapped up in my childhood. I feel she is Eleanor.
We amble on on, our friend is with us.
Near the great cedar tree there's a kind of small shrine

on a tree stump, we visit it often, it is still cared for –
a small pile of stones and shells, feathers stick out at the top,
a ring of birch branches around it. Once there were

red glass trinkets, small chains, messages on scraps of paper,
night-lights. We colour in the story – did the young couple
we once saw striding towards it lose their child, did they have

gatherings of friends there every now and then?
Ambling – our minds pottering – sunlight – stories
and yes – coming up for air.

Nightingale

           all day it seemed
and into the evening, into night – a liquid
bubbling, trills, a scoopscoopscoop of song
sustained, a lull then growing again…

           in our memory trailing with it
the place, the hot lime scent in the middle of the day,
the ash tree waving, the orchard at dusk,
its dark brambles, the smoke of our fire…

           only late at night giving way
to the rush of the river below the village,
its hum, its roar in the silent village.
But friends who knew about birds said

           it was not complete, not at all,
this song – there was no full-throated crescendo
at the end and on the cd of British Bird Sounds
it was not quite complete either…

           the bird lovers were wanting
a little more – there was still something else

Thoughts about life after a birthday lunch

for David

Though I sense the structure of it now
is ledges, hunting for nests, clinging to things
and this may be as much as we can hope for –
and yet I cannot feel that we inhabit
any present quite truly and permanently –

I remember the day...
yes it was cold and it was your birthday
and after lunch when the time had come
for the celebration walk we had talked about
so much, we wrapped up and left the pub
out into the piercing wind. Dan lent me
his jacket and the green grass was so startling,
so soft, the fields tilting, curving up,
the grass soaking us almost to our knees
and the sheep part of the landscape
with their small dots of lambs
and beyond, the steep lines of bushes...

so that moving through it all was a balm
and made the labour of the gathering seem,
in spite of punctures, taxis, cancelled trains,
light and joyous, though still
fragile, fragile and endangered.

The autumn of things

Wanting to gather up the season, live in it,
trying to, needing to turn the waste
into a sort of beauty in this thinning season –
is it remembering darning or something else –
nothing just vanishes – the power of these piles of
dead leaves and branches, the melancholy wonderful
mushroomy decaying smells of autumn?

Is this where we live?
Why not inhabit it a little like our pasts – and
like our pasts turn it into something else:
you made a sculpture – would I call it sculpture?
from a bunch of grapes' skeleton and a garlic stalk
planted on a red brown hill of bark.
The fruitfulness has gone, the skeleton stripped,
this little piece of lost pieces revives itself.

We walk here week after week in washed
blue or heavy sagging skies. The Heath is populated
with memorable ancient trees, landscapes
of oak saplings on rough hillsides, a contorted
American thorn labelled the only one in Europe –
and here and there a white tree skeleton sharply
outlined in a dark thicket. You helped me notice them.

The woman who couldn't finish things

Two friends, caught out in the rain,
 take shelter in the house of a landowner.

 After bathing from his hut on the river
(the landowner confesses he hasn't had time

to wash since spring and the water
turns first brown, then indigo around him

as he soaps himself), they sit in clean clothes
in the lamplight with the house party,

while the beautiful maid offers them
tea and jam. And the guests tell each other

stories from their lives – they each give
the storyteller their full attention

and the portraits in their gold frames
all seem to be listening too.

Among the guests is a woman who believes
she can never finish anything. When it is

her turn to tell a story she begins:
'It was the night before the European election

when nobody was talking about Europe.
Coming home, it was still light above

the dark masses of trees in the Square,
almost the longest day of the year.

The sky was green. The last email had come –
'Turn out to vote to defeat the BNP –

cascade this to friends and family.'
In the distance, at the top of the Square,

a mother was pushing a pram.
I thought of the couple who

threw themselves off Beachy Head,
threw themselves away for grief

at the death of their small son,
found in a rucksack nearby.

On the steps of the Irish Centre two small
figures, a man and a woman, faced each other

talking, lit up. In my memory they became
stooping pottery figures, pale yellow,

still archetypes. It was ten o'clock. I thought
it would be a dry, clear, chilly night.'

After her story, there is a puzzled silence.
She cannot say what her tremendous hidden

meaning is. If Anton Chekhov were here
in his imaginary company, she thinks,

he would be interested in why she
carries round a trail of half-finished

stories and poems. Would he notice
how easily her real world becomes pale,

her energy distracted, how she is not able
to decide until the moment is past

what she most wants and then
is in love with what she cannot have?

Would he say it is not so much finishing
that matters, it is the sap of the thing,

the energy, even though she has no idea
where her story is trying to take her?

When her turn comes round again,
she starts 'One evening, on my walk

along the towpath, I stopped to watch
a narrow boat slowly rising as the lock filled up.

A girl had opened the heavy lock gate and
seemed to be hunting for something on the ground.

A man with a small rucksack clambered
out of the boat and kissed her, then left

to join a party on the green sloping garden
beyond the canal where children were playing

in and out of the smoke of cooking.
I waited as the boat moved on up the canal

and there was the strangeness of seeing
Eurostar sliding past, just above it all.'

She senses a story hidden there which she cannot
grasp. Would Chekhov have said that the pace,

her words' precision, would make these small
events and fragments luminous, more complete?

Trees skies forests rivers fish would all be
consolations. Her story might begin

'It was a fine spring morning, the week before Easter.'

Notes on sources of quotations:

p18 John Keats, from his letters to Fanny Keats, 6 and 8 February 1820

p19 Joseph Severn, words he wrote on his sketch of Keats in Keats' last illness, January 1821

p21 Frank O'Hara, from his poem 'To the Film Industry in Crisis'

p45 Matthew Miles, from his poem 'On Phenomenology'

p49 Carl Dennis, from his poem 'Gravestones'

Acknowledgements

The poems in this collection are from a long stretch of time but my poetry friends and supporters have been very constant:

My warmest thanks to Jane Duran and to Mimi Khalvati for their encouragement, insights and advice in shaping the collection. And I am grateful to Robert Seatter and John Welch for reading and commenting on the final text. Many thanks, too, to Jane's Thursday Group and earlier to Mimi's Seminar for their thoughts and comments on many of the poems. Thank you, too, to members of my family and to dear friends for inspiring many of the poems. Thank you Sara and David Miles for permission to quote lines from Matt Miles' poem 'On Phenomenology' in my poem 'Matt Miles, turned away from us'. Finally, my grateful thanks to Martin Parker for the patience and thought he has put into the production of this book and the design of the cover. *SM*

Sue MacIntyre worked for many years in book publishing as an editor. Her debut poetry collection *The Wind Today* was published by Hearing Eye (2010). She has twice won first prize – for her poems 'Deep Forest' and 'Ice Sculpture' – in the Scintilla Open Poetry Competition. Earlier poems of hers were published in the pamphlet *Picnic with Seafog and Elephants* by The Many Press in 2003. Her Thumbprint pocket book *Green City* was published by Stonewood Press in 2016.

If you've enjoyed this book, help us get the word out about our books by sharing your thoughts on social media or over a lovely cuppa with friends, or by writing a review on our website or wherever you bought your copy. Thank you so much from all of us here at Stonewood Press.

www.stonewoodpress.co.uk